SECURA AIR FRYER COOKBOOK

Simple, Easy and Delicious Secura Air Fryer Recipes That Anyone Can Cook

Dane Bass

CATEGORIES

Contents

Side Dishes and Snacks 28

Poultry Recipes 38

Beef, Pork and Lamb Recipes 48

Vegetarian Recipes 56

Fish and Seafood Recipes... 71

Dessert Recipes.. 78

Introduction

Who says that you have to give up on fried food to be healthy? Well, maybe everyone, but what those people don't know is that the technology has progressed to the point where frying food and living healthy actually go hand in hand.

No, you are not dreaming, this is your dream coming true. This amazing cookbook has different finger-licking fried meals that will not raise your cholesterol levels. These mouthwatering air fryer recipes will help you get your money's worth on your air fryer, and convince you that cooking healthy doesn't have to be expensive or time consuming.

Satisfying all tastes, this cookbook will enrich your recipe folder with the yummiest breakfast, lunch, main dishes, side dishes, snacks, and dessert recipes, whether you are a vegetarian or a steak lover.

Show me one person who doesn't love crispy, deep-fried food. Even those who try to avoid fried food can sometimes find the urge to indulge irresistible. And while we all lick our plates after chowing down some delicious crunchy chicken, we are all aware that besides satisfying our taste buds, fried food brings absolutely no other benefits. In fact, it increases our bad cholesterol levels, raises our blood pressure, adds more pounds to our bodies, and makes us an unhealthy, overweight nation.

But there is more than one way to fry food. Say goodbye to eating oil-soaked and calorie-loaded unhealthy food because frying with an air fryer brings both delightful flavor and health benefits.

Now, let's healthify the American lifestyle, and enjoy our fried food without gaining weight.

Why an Air Fryer?

This revolutionized kitchen appliance fries food by blowing hot air, not by dunking it in grease. The only thing you need to do is to slightly coat the food with oil, and let the air fryer do the rest. Now, you must be thinking "but you said no oil", right? Well, here is how it works. In order for you to cook it, you need to coat your food with oil, but unlike the traditional way of frying in which the food soaks up all of the oil, the air fryer drains the grease while cooking. It has a built-in fan that circulates hot air around the food, and cooks it to perfection, soft on the inside, crispy and crunchy on the outside.

If this is not convincing enough for you to throw your old frying pans in the trash and introduce a new air fryer to your kitchen, then perhaps these next three biggest benefits of cooking with an air fryer will change your mind.

Cooking with an Air Fryer is Healthier

Food prepared in an air fryer is 80% less greasy and just as delicious, if not even better tasting, than deep-fried food. So, if you want to reduce the massive amount of fat that your favorite fried dish contains, choosing to prepare it in an air fryer is your healthier option. Frying with an air fryer will help you lose weight without sacrificing the satisfaction and comfort of fried food.

Cooking with an Air Fryer is Faster

Do you know what the best part about an air fryer is? You don't have to spend your time waiting for it to heat to the right temperature in order to start cooking. The air fryer can come from room temperature to more than 300 degrees F in less than 3 minutes. This is a real time-saver when it comes to cooking. We all know how long it takes for a large amount of oil to heat to the appropriate temperature for us to start deep-frying. Air fryers are also much faster than your traditional oven.

Cooking with an Air Fryer is Cleaner

Aren't you tired of scrubbing all that sticky grease from the bottom of your frying pan? Or cleaning grease splatters off your stove? If so, then cooking with an air fryer will be a real enjoyment for you. Since there is literary no grease, the air fryer cleaning process is super convenient. All parts of the air fryer are easily removable and most importantly, dishwasher safe. The best way to clean it is to it with hot water and a few drops of liquid dishwasher. Let it soak for a couple of minutes, and then clean it with a non-abrasive sponge. Rinse under water, and voila.

And even though fried food prepared in an air fryer tastes amazing the best part is that you can use your air fryer for so much more than making French fries. You can even prepare baked goods or roast your chicken in it.

An air fryer is super versatile and once you get the handle of cooking with this amazing kitchen appliance, you will see that oil-free cooking can really be limitless.

Here are some general air fryer cooking tips:
- Don't overcrowd the basket of the air fryer to ensure even cooking.
- You can insert any baking dish or bowl, as long as they fit in the air fryer.
- You can use aluminum foil and parchment paper just like when cooking in the oven.
- You can open the air fryer to check the doneness of the food, as many times as you like, just like you do with your oven.
- Flip the food halfway through to ensure even crispiness.
- Shake the basket of your air fryer instead of stirring frequently.
- Adding water to the drawer of the air fryer can prevent the food getting too smoky.
- You can use your air fryer to reheat food, as well.
- Now, read these recipes and see how the air fryer is the perfect substitute for your stove and oven.

Breakfast Recipes

Onion and Cheese Omelet

(Prep + Cook Time: 12 - 15 minutes / Servings: 1)

Nutritional info per serving:

Calories 347.3, Carbohydrates 6 g, Fat 23.2 g, Protein 13.6 g

Ingredients:

2 eggs

2 tbsp. grated cheddar cheese

1 tsp. soy sauce

½ onion, sliced

¼ tsp. pepper

1 tbsp. olive oil

Directions:

1. Whisk the eggs along with the pepper and soy sauce.

2. Preheat the secura air fryer to 350 degrees F. Heat the olive oil and add the egg mixture and the onion. Cook for 8 to 10 minutes. Top with the grated cheddar cheese.

Creamy Zucchini Muffins

(Prep + Cook Time: 20 minutes / Servings: 4)

Nutritional info per serving:

Calories 357, Carbohydrates 47.6 g, Fat 13 g, Protein 12.6 g

Ingredients:

1 ½ cups flour

1 tsp. cinnamon

3 eggs

2 tsp. baking powder

2 tbsp. sugar

1 cup milk

2 tbsp. butter, melted

1 tbsp. yogurt

½ cup shredded zucchini

Pinch of salt

2 tbsp. cream cheese

Directions:

1. Preheat the secura air fryer to 350 degrees F.
2. In a bowl, whisk the eggs along with the sugar, salt, cinnamon, cream cheese, flour, and baking powder.
3. In another bowl, combine all of the liquid ingredients.
4. Gently combine the dry and liquid mixtures. Stir in zucchini.
5. Line the muffin tins and pour the batter into the tins.
6. Cook for 12 minutes.
7. Check with a toothpick.
8. You may need to cook them for additional 2 to 3 minutes.

Toasted Herb and Garlic Bagel

(Prep + Cook Time: 6 minutes / Servings: 1)

Nutritional info per serving:

Calories 432, Carbohydrates 40.4 g, Fat 25.7 g, Protein 10.4 g

Ingredients:

2 tbsp. butter, softened
1 tsp. dried basil
1 tsp. dried parsley
1 tsp. garlic powder

1 tbsp. Parmesan cheese
Salt and pepper, to taste
1 bagel

Directions:

1. Preheat the secura air fryer to 370 degrees. Cut the bagel in half.
2. Place in the air fryer and cook for 3 minutes.
3. Combine the butter, Parmesan, garlic, basil, and parsley in a small bowl.
4. Season with salt and pepper, to taste. Spread the mixture onto the toasted bagel.
5. Return the bagel to the secura air fryer and cook for additional 3 minutes.

Raspberry and Vanilla Pancakes

(Prep + Cook Time: 15 minutes / Servings: 4)

Nutritional info per serving:

Calories 483, Carbohydrates 108 g, Fat 4.8 g, Protein 13.5 g

Ingredients:

2 cups all-purpose flour

1 cup milk

3 eggs, beaten

1 tsp. baking powder

1 cup brown sugar

1 ½ tsp. vanilla extract

½ cup frozen raspberries, thawed

2 tbsp. maple syrup

Pinch of salt

Cooking spray or butter for greasing

Directions:

1. Preheat the secura air fryer to 390 degrees F.

2. In a bowl, mix the flour, baking powder, salt, milk, eggs, vanilla extract, sugar, and maple syrup, until smooth.

3. Stir in the raspberries. Do it gently to avoid coloring the batter.

4. Grease a baking dish or spray it with cooking spray.

5. Drop the batter onto the dish. Just make sure to leave some space between the pancakes. If there is some batter left (I used it all in a single batch), repeat the process.

6. Cook for 10 minutes.

7. Enjoy.

Crustless Mediterranean Quiche

(Prep + Cook Time: 40 minutes / Servings: 2)

Nutritional info per serving:

Calories 540.1, Carbohydrates 10.8 g, Fat 43.9g, Protein 25.8 g

Ingredients:

4 eggs
½ cup chopped tomatoes
1 cup crumbled feta cheese
1 tbsp. chopped basil
1 tbsp. chopped oregano

¼ cup chopped kalamata olives
¼ cup chopped onion
2 tbsp. olive oil
½ cup milk
Salt and pepper to taste

Directions:

1. Preheat the air fryer to 340 degrees F. Brush a pie pan with the olive oil.
2. Beat the eggs along with the milk and some salt and pepper.
3. Stir in all of the remaining ingredients.
4. Pour the egg mixture into the pan. Cook for 30 minutes.

Prosciutto, Mozzarella and Egg in a Cup

(Prep + Cook Time: 20 minutes / Servings: 2)

Nutritional info per serving:

Calories 291.3, Carbohydrates 12.9 g, Fat 20.5 g, Protein 13 g

Ingredients:

2 slices of bread
2 prosciutto slices, chopped
2 eggs
4 tomato slices
¼ tsp. balsamic vinegar
2 tbsp. grated mozzarella

¼ tsp. maple syrup
2 tbsp. mayonnaise
Salt and pepper, to taste
Cooking spray or butter for greasing

Directions:

1. Preheat the air fryer to 320 degrees.
2. Grease two large ramekins.
3. Place one bread slice in the bottom of each ramekin.
4. Arrange 2 tomato slices on top of each bread slice.
5. Divide the mozzarella between the ramekins.
6. Crack the eggs over the mozzarella.
7. Drizzle with maple syrup and balsamic vinegar.
8. Season with some salt and pepper.
9. Cook for 10 minutes, or until desired.
10. Top with mayonnaise.

Three Meat Cheesy Omelet

(Prep + Cook Time: 20 minutes / Servings: 2)

Nutritional info per serving:

Calories 590, Carbohydrates 6.1 g, Fat 42.5 g, Protein 44 g

Ingredients:

1 beef sausage, chopped
4 slices prosciutto, chopped
3 oz. salami, chopped
1 cup grated mozzarella cheese

4 eggs
1 tbsp. chopped onion
1 tbsp. ketchup

Directions:

1. Preheat the air fryer to 350 degrees F.
2. Whisk the eggs with the ketchup in a bowl. Stir in the onion.
3. Brown the sausage in the air fryer for about 2 minutes.
4. Meanwhile, combine the egg mixture, mozzarella cheese, salami and prosciutto.
5. Pour the egg mixture over the sausage and give it a stir. Cook for about 10 minutes.

Air Fried Shirred Eggs

(Prep + Cook Time: 20 minutes / Servings: 2)

Nutritional info per serving:

Calories 279.9, Carbohydrates 1.8 g, Fat 20 g, Protein 20.8 g

Ingredients:

2 tsp. butter, for greasing
4 eggs, divided
2 tbsp. heavy cream
4 slices of ham

3 tbsp. Parmesan cheese
¼ tsp. paprika
¼ tsp. pepper
2 tsp. chopped chives

Directions:

1. Preheat the air fryer to 320 degrees F. Grease a pie pan with the butter.
2. Arrange the ham slices on the bottom of the pan to cover it completely. Use more slices if needed (or less if your pan is smaller).
3. Whisk one egg along with the heavy cream, salt and pepper, in a small bowl.
4. Pour the mixture over the ham slices. Crack the other eggs over the ham.
5. Sprinkle the Parmesan cheese. Cook for 14 minutes.
6. Sprinkle with paprika and garnish with chives.
7. Serve with bread.

The Simplest Grilled Cheese

(Prep + Cook Time: 10 minutes / Servings: 1)

Nutritional info per serving:

Calories 452, Carbohydrates 23 g, Fat 32.3 g, Protein 17 g

Ingredients:

2 tsp. butter
2 slices of bread

3 slices of American cheese

Directions:

1. Preheat the air fryer to 370 degrees F.
2. Spread one teaspoon of butter on the outside of each of the bread.
3. Place the cheese on the inside of one bread slice.
4. Top with the other slice.
5. Cook in the air fryer for 4 minutes.
6. Flip the sandwich over and cook for additional 4 minutes.
7. Serve cut diagonally.

Very Berry Breakfast Puff

(Prep + Cook Time: 20 minutes / Servings: 3)

Nutritional info per serving:

Calories 255.9, Carbohydrates 24.5 g, Fat 15.7 g, Protein 4.3 g

Ingredients:

3 pastry dough sheets

2 tbsp. mashed strawberries

2 tbsp. mashed raspberries

¼ tsp. vanilla extract

2 cups cream cheese

1 tbsp. honey

Directions:

1. Preheat the air fryer to 375 degrees F.
2. Divide the cream cheese between the dough sheets and spread it evenly.
3. In a small bowl combine the berries, honey and vanilla.
4. Divide the mixture between the pastry sheets.
5. Pinch the ends of the sheets, to form puff.
6. You can seal them by brushing some water onto the edges, or even better, use egg wash.
7. Place the puffs on a lined baking dish.
8. Place in the air fryer and cook for 15 minutes.

Sweet Bread Pudding with Raisins

(Prep + Cook Time: 45 minutes / Servings: 3)

Nutritional info per serving:

Calories 529.6, Carbohydrates 77 g, Fat 20 g, Protein 13 g

Ingredients:

8 slices of bread
½ cup buttermilk
¼ cup honey
1 cup milk
2 eggs
½ tsp. vanilla extract

2 tbsp. butter, softened
¼ cup sugar
4 tbsp. raisins
2 tbsp. chopped hazelnuts
Cinnamon for garnish

Directions:

1. Preheat the air fryer to 310 degrees F.
2. Beat the eggs along with the buttermilk, honey, milk, vanilla, sugar and butter.
3. Stir in raisins and hazelnuts. Cut the bread into cubes and place it in a bowl.
4. Pour the milk mixture over the bread.
5. Let soak for about 10 minutes.
6. Cook the bread pudding for 30 minutes.
7. Garnish with cinnamon.

Lunch Recipes

Avocado and Chicken Lunch

(Prep + Cook Time: 20 minutes / Servings: 2)

Nutritional info per serving:

Calories 356, Carbohydrates 7.9 g, Fat 19.3 g, Protein 39.3 g

Ingredients:

12 oz. chicken breasts
1 avocado, sliced
4 radishes, sliced

1 tbsp. chopped parsley
Salt and pepper, to taste

Directions:

1. Preheat the air fryer to 300 degrees F.
2. Cut the chicken into small cubes.
3. Combine all of the ingredients in a bowl.
4. Transfer to a baking dish.
5. Cook for about 14 minutes.

Carbonara and Mushroom Spaghetti

(Prep + Cook Time: 30 minutes / Servings: 4)

Nutritional info per serving:

Calories 395.7, Carbohydrates 57.9 g, Fat 13 g, Protein 13 g

Ingredients:

½ lb. white button mushrooms, sliced
½ cup of water
1 tsp. butter
2 garlic cloves, chopped

12 oz. spaghetti, cooked
14 oz. carbonara mushroom sauce (store bought)
Salt and pepper, to taste

Directions:

1. Preheat the air fryer to 300 degrees F. Add the butter and garlic and cook for 3 minutes. Add the mushrooms and cook for 5 more minutes.
2. Stir in mushroom carbonara sauce and water. Season with salt and pepper.
3. Cook for 18 minutes. Stir in the spaghetti and cook for 1 minute more.

Egg Rolls

(Prep + Cook Time: 18 minutes / Servings: 3)

Nutritional info per serving:

Calories 574.5, Carbohydrates 51 g, Fat 27.4 g, Protein 28.3 g

Ingredients:

1 package egg roll wrappers (12 wrappers)
1 cup cooked ground beef
1 large grated carrot

1 cup grated mozzarella cheese
2 tsp. olive oil
¼ tsp. salt
¼ tsp. pepper

Directions:

1. Preheat the air fryer to 370 degrees F.
2. In a bowl, combine the beef, carrot, mozzarella, salt, and pepper.
3. Place the egg roll sheets on a dry and clean surface.
4. Divide the beef mixture between them.
5. Roll up the egg rolls.
6. Place the olive oil in the air fryer.
7. Arrange the egg rolls and cook for 13 minutes.
8. Enjoy.

Cheat Hawaiian Pizza

(Prep + Cook Time: 15 minutes / Servings: 2)

Nutritional info per serving:

Calories 425.1, Carbohydrates 50.2 g, Fat 15.3 g, Protein 23.8 g

Ingredients:

2 tortillas

8 ham slices

8 mozzarella slices

8 thin pineapple slices

2 tbsp. tomato sauce

1 tsp. dried parsley

Directions:

1. Preheat the air fryer to 330 degrees F.

2. Spread the tomato sauce onto the tortillas.

3. Arrange 4 ham slices on each tortilla.

4. Top the ham with the pineapple.

5. Top the pizza with mozzarella.

6. Sprinkle the parsley over.

7. Cook for 10 minutes.

8. Enjoy.

Grilled Apple and Brie Sandwich

(Prep + Cook Time: 8 - 10 minutesServing: 1)

Nutritional info per serving:

Calories 391.6, Carbohydrates 27.8 g, Fat 25.9 g, Protein 18 g

Ingredients:

2 bread slices

½ apple, thinly sliced

2 tsp. butter

2 oz. brie cheese, thinly sliced

Directions:

1. Preheat the air fryer to 350 degrees F.
2. Spread the butter on the outside of the bread slices.
3. Arrange the apple slices on the inside of one bread slice.
4. Place the brie slices on top of the apple.
5. Top with the other slice of bread.
6. Cook for 5 minutes.
7. Serve cut diagonally.

Ham and Mozzarella Eggplant Boats

(Prep + Cook Time: 17 minutes / Servings: 2)

Nutritional info per serving:

Calories 323.1, Carbohydrates 15.7 g, Fat 16.4 g, Protein 28.3 g

Ingredients:

1 eggplant
4 ham slices, chopped
1 cup shredded mozzarella cheese, divid-

ed
1 tsp. dried parsley
Salt and pepper, to taste

Directions:

1. Preheat the air fryer to 330 degrees F.
2. Peel the eggplant and cut it lengthwise in half.
3. Scoop some of the flash out.
4. Season with salt and pepper.
5. Divide half the mozzarella cheese between the eggplants.
6. Place the ham on top of the mozzarella.
7. Top with the remaining mozzarella cheese.
8. Sprinkle with parsley.
9. Cook for 12 minutes.

Leftover Turkey and Mushroom Sandwich

(Prep + Cook Time: 15 minutes / Servings: 1)

Nutritional info per serving:

Calories 318.3, Carbohydrates 25.6 g, Fat 16.4 g, Protein 18.4 g

Ingredients:

⅓ cup shredded leftover turkey
⅓ cup sliced mushrooms
1 tbsp. butter, divided
2 tomato slices

½ tsp. red pepper flakes
¼ tsp. salt
¼ tsp. black pepper
1 hamburger bun

Directions:

1. Preheat the air fryer to 350 degrees F. Melt half of the butter and add the mushrooms. Cook for about 4 minutes.
2. Meanwhile, cut the bun in half and spread the remaining butter on the outside of the bun. Place the turkey on one half of the bun.
3. Arrange the mushroom slices on top of the turkey. Place the tomato slices on top of the mushrooms. Sprinkle with salt pepper and red pepper flakes.
4. Top with the other bun half. Cook for 5 minutes.

Garlicky Chicken on Green Bed

(Prep + Cook Time: 20 minutes / Servings: 1)

Nutritional info per serving:

Calories 551, Carbohydrates 10.7 g, Fat 45 g, Protein 28.7 g

Ingredients:

½ cup baby spinach leaves
½ cup shredded romaine
3 large kale leaves, chopped
4 oz. chicken breasts, cut into cubes

3 tbsp. olive oil, divided
1 tsp. balsamic vinegar
1 garlic clove, minced
Salt and pepper, to taste

Directions:

1. Preheat the air fryer to 390 degrees F.
2. Place the chicken in a bowl along with 1 tbsp. olive oil and garlic Season with some salt and pepper and toss to combine.
3. Place on a lined baking dish and cook for 14 minutes.
4. Meanwhile, place the greens in a large bowl.
5. Add the remaining olive oil and balsamic vinegar.
6. Season with some salt and pepper and toss to combine.
7. Top with the chicken.
8. Enjoy.

Crispy Prosciutto and Feta Quinoa Salad

(Prep + Cook Time: 10 minutes / Servings: 2)

Nutritional info per serving:

Calories 533.8, Carbohydrates 62.9 g, Fat 22.7 g, Protein 21.6 g

Ingredients:

1 cup cooked quinoa
½ cup crumbled feta cheese
¼ cup chopped olives
2 prosciutto slices, chopped

1 tsp. olive oil
½ red bell pepper, chopped
Salt and pepper, to taste

Directions:

1. Preheat the air fryer to 350 degrees F.
2. Place the olive oil and pepper and cook for 2 minutes.
3. Add the prosciutto and cook for 3 more minutes.
4. Meanwhile, combine the quinoa, feta, and olives, in an ovenproof bowl.
5. Stir in cooked prosciutto and peppers, and season with some salt and pepper.
6. Place the bowl in the basket of the air fryer and cook for 1 minute.

Italian Sausage Patties

(Prep + Cook Time: 20 minutes / Servings: 4)

Nutritional info per serving:

Calories 332.3 Carbohydrates 6.2 g, Fat 24.6 g, Protein 18.6 g

Ingredients:

1 lb. ground Italian sausage
¼ cup breadcrumbs
1 tsp. dried parsley
1 tsp. red pepper Flakes

½ tsp. salt
¼ tsp. black pepper
¼ tsp. garlic powder
1 egg, beaten

Directions:

1. Preheat the air fryer to 350 degrees F.

2. Combine all of the ingredients in a large bowl.

3. Line a baking sheet with parchment paper.

4. Make patties out of the sausage mixture and arrange them on the baking sheet.

5. Cook for about 15 minutes.

6. Serve as desired (they are amazing with tzatziki sauce).

7. Enjoy.

Side Dishes and Snacks

Crispy Eggplant Fries

(Prep + Cook Time: 20 minutes / Servings: 2)

Nutritional info per serving:

Calories 87, Carbohydrates 11.1 g, Fat 5.8 g, Protein 1.3 g

Ingredients:

2 eggplants
⅓ cup olive oil
⅓ cup cornstarch

½ cup water
a pinch of salt
1 cup of tomato sauce or yogurt, optional

Directions:

1. Preheat the Air Fryer to 370°F. Cut the eggplants in slices of ½ -inch each.
2. In a big bowl, mix the cornstarch, water, olive oil, and the eggplants.
3. Carefully coat the eggplants. Then cook them in the Air Fryer for around 15 minutes or until the eggplant starts to brown.
4. Repeat the process until all eggplant slices are fried.
5. Serve with yogurt or tomato sauce!

Crispy Parsnip Fries

(Prep + Cook Time: 15 minutes / Servings: 3)

Nutritional info per serving:

Calories 83, Carbohydrates 13.1 g, Fat 5.5 g, Protein 2.1 g

Ingredients:

6 large parsnips
⅓ cup olive oil

⅓ cup cornstarch
⅓ cup water

Directions:

1. Preheat the Air Fryer to 390° F.
2. Peel and cut the parsnips to ½ inch by 3 inches.
3. Mix the cornstarch, the olive oil, the water and the parsnips in a large bowl.
4. Combine the ingredients and coat the parsnips.
5. Fry the parsnips for around 12 minutes.

Crispy Cauliflower with Pine Nuts and Raisins

(Prep + Cook Time: 23 minutes / Servings: 4)

Nutritional info per serving:

Calories 165, Carbohydrates 32 g, Fat 6 g, Protein 4 g

Ingredients:

1 head of cauliflower
⅓ cup olive oil
⅓ cup golden raisins

⅓ cup toasted pine nuts
1 cup hot water
a pinch of salt

Directions:

1. Preheat the Air Fryer to 380°F and add the oil and the pine nuts. Cook for 2 minutes, then set aside.
2. In a medium bowl, pour 1 cup of hot water and add the raisins. Then set aside. Core the head of the cauliflower using a knife and cut it into medium-sized pieces.
3. In a pan, boil 5 cups of water and add the cut florets and leave them there until the water boils again.
4. Remove the cauliflower florets from the pan and transfer them to a large bowl.
5. Add the olive oil and the salt. Place about half of the florets in the preheated Air Fryer and cook them for 10-12 minutes.
6. Repeat the process with the rest of the cauliflower florets.
7. Drain the raisins in a strainer. and toss them over the florets and the pine nuts.

Buttermilk Onion Rings

(Prep + Cook Time: 30 minutes / Servings: 4)

Nutritional info per serving:

Calories 257, Carbohydrates 49.1 g, Fat 3 g, Protein 10.6 g

Ingredients:

2 sweet onions
2 cups buttermilk
2 cups pancake mix

2 cups water
1 package cornbread mix
1 tsp. salt

Directions:

1. Preheat the air fryer to 370 degrees F. Slice the onions into rings.
2. Combine the pancake mix with the water.
3. Line a baking sheet with parchment paper.
4. Dip the rings in the cornbread mixture first, and then in the pancake batter.
5. Place half of the onion rings onto the sheet and then into the air fryer.
6. Air fry for 8 to 12 minutes. Repeat one more time.
7. Serve with your favorite dipping or as a side dish.

Grilled Watermelon and Minty Cheese

(Prep + Cook Time: 15 minutes / Servings: 4)

Nutritional info per serving:

Calories 246, Carbohydrates 3.3 g, Fat 16.5 g, Protein 12.8 g

Ingredients:

8 thick watermelon slices
12 kalamata olives
8 oz. halloumi cheese
2 tbsp. chopped parsley

2 tbsp. chopped mint
Juice and zest of 1 lemon
Salt and pepper, to taste
Olive oil

Directions:

1. Preheat the air fryer to 350 degrees F.
2. Season the watermelon with some salt and pepper and gently brush them with olive oil.
3. Place in the air fryer and cook for about 4 minutes.
4. Brush the cheese with olive oil and place it in the air fryer. Cook for 4 minutes.
5. Place them on a platter and serve with olives and sprinkled with herbs, and lemon zest and juice.

Mashed Potato Balls

(Prep + Cook Time: 22 minutes / Servings: 6)

Nutritional info per serving:

Calories 528, Carbohydrates 76.4 g, Fat 17.8 g, Protein 21 g

Ingredients:

1 cup flour
1 cup breadcrumbs
4 cups mashed potatoes
3 eggs, beaten
3 oz. softened cream cheese

½ cup Parmesan cheese
2 tbsp. chopped chives
¼ tsp. pepper
½ tsp. garlic powder
½ tsp. salt

Directions:

1. Preheat the air fryer to 330 degrees.
2. In a large bowl, combine the mashed potatoes, cream cheese, salt, pepper, garlic powder, chives and Parmesan cheese.
3. Form 16 balls out of the mixture.
4. Dip each bowl into the flour, then into the egg, and finally coat with the breadcrumbs.
5. Arrange half of the balls onto a lined baking sheet.
6. Cook for 7 minutes. Repeat with the other half.

Air Fried Pin Wheels

(Prep + Cook Time: 50 minutes / Servings: 6)

Nutritional info per serving:

Calories 411, Carbohydrates 19.9 g, Fat 28.4 g, Protein 17.7 g

Ingredients:

1 sheet puff pastry

8 ham slices

1 ½ cups Gruyere cheese, grated

4 tsp. Dijon mustard

Directions:

1. Preheat the air fryer to 370 degrees F.
2. Place the pastry on a lightly floured flat surface.
3. Brush the mustard over and then arrange the ham slices. Top with the cheese.
4. Start at the shorter edge and roll up the pastry.
5. Wrap it in a plastic foil and place in the freezer for about half an hour, until it becomes firm and easy to cut. Meanwhile, slice the pastry into 6 rounds.
6. Line a baking sheet with parchment paper and arrange the pinwheels on top.
7. Cook for 10 minutes.

Cumin Baby Carrots

(Prep + Cook Time: 25 minutes / Servings: 4)

Nutritional info per serving:

Calories 124.1, Carbohydrates 13.7 g, Fat 6.9 g, Protein 1.8 g

Ingredients:

1 ¼ lb. baby carrots

2 tbsp. olive oil

1 tsp. cumin seeds

½ tsp. cumin powder

½ tsp. garlic powder

1 handful cilantro, chopped

1 tsp. salt

½ tsp. black pepper

Directions:

1. Preheat the air fryer to 370 degrees F. Place the baby carrots in a large bowl.
2. Add cumin seeds, cumin, olive oil, salt, garlic powder, and pepper, and stir to coat them well.
3. Place the baby carrots in the basket of the air fryer and cook for 20 minutes.
4. Place on a platter and sprinkle with chopped cilantro.

Crispy Cheesy Straws

(Prep + Cook Time: 45 minutes / Servings: 8)

Nutritional info per serving:

Calories 121.9, Carbohydrates 8.4 g, Fat 7.2 g, Protein 7.2 g

Ingredients:

2 cups cauliflower florets, steamed
1 egg
3 ½ oz. oats
1 red onion, diced

1 tsp. mustard
5 oz. cheddar cheese
Salt and pepper, to taste

Directions:

1. Preheat the air fryer to 350 degrees F.
2. Place the oats in a food processor and process until they are the consistency of breadcrumbs. You can also use regular breadcrumbs for this recipe and omit the oats, if you prefer. I find it yummier this way.
3. Place the steamed florets in a cheesecloth and squeeze out the excess liquid. Place the florets in a large bowl. Add the rest of the ingredients to the bowl.
4. Mix well with your hands to combine the ingredients completely.
5. Take a little bit of the mixture and twist it into a straw.
6. Place on a lined baking sheet. Repeat with the rest of the mixture. Cook for 10 minutes.
7. Turn them over and cook for additional 10 minutes.

Nutty and Zesty Brussels Sprouts with Raisins

(Prep + Cook Time: 40 - 45 minutes / Servings: 4)

Nutritional info per serving:

Calories 210.8, Carbohydrates 22.1 g, Fat 13.5 g, Protein 5.1 g

Ingredients:

14 oz. Brussels sprouts, steamed
2 oz. raisins
1 tbsp. olive oil

Juice and zest of 1 orange
2 oz. toasted pine nuts

Directions:

1. Soak the raisins in the orange juice and let sit for about 20 minutes.
2. Preheat the air fryer to 370 degrees F.
3. Drizzle the Brussels sprouts with the olive oil and place them in the basket of the air fryer.
4. Cook for 15 minutes.
5. Place in a bowl and top with pine nuts, raisins and orange zest.
6. Enjoy.

Asparagus Fries

(Prep + Cook Time: 30 minutes / Servings: 6)

Nutritional info per serving:

Calories 171.5, Carbohydrates 21.2 g, Fat 5.3 g, Protein 10.5 g

Ingredients:

1 lb. asparagus spears
¼ cup flour
1 cup breadcrumbs

½ cup Parmesan cheese, grated
2 eggs, beaten
Salt and pepper, to taste

Directions:

1. Preheat the air fryer to 370 degrees.
2. Combine the breadcrumbs and Parmesan in a small bowl. Season with some salt and pepper.
3. Line a baking sheet with parchment paper.
4. Dip half of the asparagus spears into the flour first, then into the eggs, and finally coat with breadcrumbs.
5. Arrange them on the sheet and bake for about 8 to 10 minutes.
6. Repeat with the other half of the spears.
7. Enjoy.

Garlic and Rosemary Mushrooms

(Prep + Cook Time: 20 minutes / Servings: 4)

Nutritional info per serving:

Calories 123.6, Carbohydrates 3.5 g, Fat 11.8 g, Protein 2.8 g

Ingredients:

2 rosemary sprigs
12 oz. white button mushrooms
¼ cup melted butter

½ tsp. salt
¼ tsp. black pepper
3 garlic cloves, minced

Directions:

1. Preheat the air fryer to 350 degrees F.
2. Wash and pat dry the mushrooms. The cut them in half.
3. Place them in a large bowl.
4. Add the remaining ingredients to the bowl and toss well to combine.
5. Transfer the mushrooms to the basket of the air fryer.
6. Cook for 12 minutes.
7. Enjoy.

Cauliflower and Cheddar Tater Tots

(Prep + Cook Time: 35 minutes / Servings: 10)

Nutritional info per serving:

Calories 111.8, Carbohydrates 10.9 g, Fat 5.2 g, Protein 6.4 g

Ingredients:

2 lb. cauliflower florets, steamed
5 oz. cheddar cheese
1 onion, diced
1 cup breadcrumbs
1 egg, beaten

1 tsp. chopped parsley
1 tsp. chopped oregano
1 tsp. chopped chives
1 tsp. garlic powder
Salt and pepper, to taste

Directions:

1. Mash the cauliflower and place it in a large bowl.
2. Add the onion, parsley, oregano, chives, garlic powder, some salt and pepper, and cheddar cheese. Mix with your hands until fully combined.
3. Form 12 balls out of the mixture. Line a baking sheet with paper.
4. Dip half of the tater tots into the egg and then coat with breadcrumbs.
5. Arrange them on the baking sheet and cook in the air fryer at 350 minutes for 15 minutes. Repeat with the other half.

Blooming Buttery Onion

(Prep + Cook Time: 40 minutes / Servings: 4)

Nutritional info per serving:

Calories 173.4, Carbohydrates 9.5 g, Fat 15.1 g, Protein 1.4 g

Ingredients:

4 onions
4 butter dollops
1 tbsp. olive oil

Directions:

1. Peel the onions and slice off the root bottom so it can sit well.
2. Cut slices into the onion to make it look like a blooming flower, juts make sure not to go all the way through. Four cuts will do.
3. Preheat the air fryer to 350 degrees F.
4. Place the onions in the air fryer.
5. Drizzle with olive oil.
6. Place a dollop of butter on top of each onion.
7. Cook for about 30 minutes.
8. Enjoy.

Parmesan Cabbage Side Dish

(Prep + Cook Time: 30 minutes / Servings: 4)

Nutritional info per serving:

Calories 245, Carbohydrates 7.4 g, Fat 19.4 g, Protein 12.2 g

Ingredients:

½ head of cabbage, cut into 4 wedges
4 tbsp. butter, melted
2 cup Parmesan cheese

Salt and pepper, to taste
1 tsp. smoked paprika

Directions:

1. Preheat the air fryer to 330 degrees F. Line a baking sheet with parchment paper.
2. Brush the butter over the cabbage wedges. Season with some salt and pepper.
3. Coat the cabbage with the Parmesan cheese.
4. Arrange on the baking sheet. Sprinkle with paprika over.
5. Cook for 15 minutes, then flip the wedges over and cook for additional 10 minutes.
6. Enjoy.

Tom Yum Wings

(Prep + Cook Time: 4 hours 20 minutes / Servings: 2)

Nutritional info per serving:

Calories 287, Carbohydrates 20 g, Fat 7 g, Protein 26 g

Ingredients:

8 chicken wings
1 tbsp. water
2 tbsp. potato starch

2 tbsp. cornstarch
2 tbsp. tom yum paste
½ tsp. baking powder

Directions:

1. Combine the tom yum paste and water, in a small bowl.
2. Place the wings in a large bowl, add the tom yum mixture and coat well.
3. Cover the bowl and refrigerate for 4 hours.
4. Preheat the air fryer to 370 degrees.
5. Meanwhile, combine the baking powder, cornstarch and potato starch.
6. Dip each wing in the starch mixture.
7. Place on a lined baking dish in the air fryer and cook for 7 minutes.
8. Flip over and cook for 5 to 7 minutes more.

Cordon Bleu Chicken

(Prep + Cook Time: 40 minutes / Servings: 4)

Nutritional info per serving:

Calories 317, Carbohydrates 48 g, Fat 22 g, Protein 35 g

Ingredients:

4 skinless and boneless chicken breasts
4 slices ham
4 slices Swiss cheese
3 tbsp. all-purpose flour
4 tbsp. butter

1 tsp. paprika
1 tsp. chicken bouillon granules
½ cup dry white wine
1 cup heavy whipping cream
1 tbsp. cornstarch

Directions:

1. Preheat the Air Fryer to 380° F.
2. Pound the chicken breasts and put a slice of ham on each of the chicken breasts.
3. Fold the edges of the chicken over the filling and secure the edges with toothpicks.
4. In a medium bowl, combine the paprika and the flour and coat the chicken pieces.
5. Fry the chicken for 20 minutes. In a large skillet, heat the butter and add the bouillon and the wine. Reduce the heat to low.
6. Remove the chicken from the Air Fryer and place it in the skillet. Let simmer for around 20-25 minutes.

Chicken with Prunes

(Prep + Cook Time: 55 minutes / Servings: 6)

Nutritional info per serving:

Calories 288, Carbohydrates 44 g, Fat 18 g, Protein 39 g

Ingredients:

1 whole chicken, 3 lb.
½ cup of pitted prunes

3 minced cloves of garlic
2 tbsp. of capers

2 bay leaves

2 tbsp. red wine vinegar

2 tbsp. of olive oil

1 tbsp. of dried oregano

¼ cup of packed brown sugar

1 tbsp. of chopped and fresh parsley

salt and black pepper

Directions:

1. In a big and deep bowl, mix the prunes, the olives, the capers, the garlic, the olive oil, the bay leaves, the oregano, the vinegar, salt and pepper.

2. Spread the mixture on the bottom of a baking tray, and place the chicken.

3. Preheat the Air Fryer to 360° F. Sprinkle a little bit of brown sugar on top of the chicken and cook for 55 minutes. Garnish with fresh parsley.

Rosemary Lemon Chicken

(Prep + Cook Time: 60 minutes / Servings: 2)

Nutritional info per serving:

Calories 275, Carbohydrates 19 g, Fat 7.6 g, Protein 36 g

Ingredients:

2 chicken breasts

1 tsp. minced ginger

2 rosemary sprigs

½ lemon, cut into wedges

1 tbsp. soy sauce

½ tbsp. olive oil

1 tbsp. oyster sauce

3 tbsp. brown sugar

Directions:

1. Place the ginger, soy sauce, and olive oil in a bowl. Add the chicken and coat well.

2. Cover the bowl and refrigerate for 30 minutes.

3. Preheat the air fryer to 370 degrees F.

4. Transfer the marinated chicken into a baking dish. Cook for about 6 minutes.

5. Meanwhile, mix the oyster sauce, rosemary and brown sugar in a small bowl.

6. Pour the sauce over the chicken. Arrange the lemon wedges in the dish.

7. Return to the air fryer and cook for 13 more minutes.

Simple Panko Turkey

(Prep + Cook Time: 25 minutes / Servings: 6)

Nutritional info per serving:

Calories 286, Carbohydrates 6.6 g, Fat 18 g, Protein 24 g

Ingredients:

6 turkey breasts, boneless and skinless
2 cups panko1 tsp. salt
½ tsp. cayenne pepper

½ tsp. black pepper
1 stick butter, melted

Directions:

1. In a bowl, combine the panko, half of the black pepper, the cayenne pepper, and half of the salt.
2. In another small bowl, combine the melted butter with salt and pepper. Don't add salt if you use salted butter.
3. Brush the butter mixture over the turkey breast.
4. Coat the turkey with the panko mixture.
5. Arrange them on a lined baking dish.
6. Air fry for about 15 minutes at 390 degrees F. If the turkey breasts are thinner, cook only for 8 minutes.

Greek-Style Chicken

(Prep + Cook Time: 45 minutes / Servings: 6)

Nutritional info per serving:

Calories 283, Carbohydrates 34 g, Fat 12 g, Protein 27 g

Ingredients:

1 whole chicken, around 3 lb., cut in pieces

3 chopped cloves of garlic
½ cup of olive oil

100 ml of white wine

1 tbsp. of fresh rosemary

1 tbsp. of chopped fresh oregano

1 tbsp. of fresh thyme

juice from 1 lemon

salt and black pepper, to taste

Directions:

1. In a large bowl, combine the cloves of garlic, the rosemary, the thyme, the olive oil, the lemon juice, the oregano, salt and pepper.
2. Mix all ingredients very well and spread the mixture into a baking dish.
3. Add the chicken and stir.
4. Preheat the Air Fryer to 380° F and transfer in the chicken mixture.
5. Sprinkle with white wine and cook for 45 minutes.

Chicken Quarters with Broccoli and Rice

(Prep + Cook Time: 60 minutes / Servings: 3)

Nutritional info per serving:

Calories 256, Carbohydrates 29 g, Fat 15 g, Protein 23 g

Ingredients:

3 chicken leg quarters

1 package instant long grain rice

1 cup chopped broccoli

2 cups water

1 can of condensed cream chicken soup

1 tbsp. minced garlic

Directions:

1. Preheat the Air Fryer to 390° F and place the chicken quarters in the Air Fryer.
2. Season with salt, pepper and a tbsp. of oil and cook for 30 minutes.
3. Meanwhile, in a deep large bowl and mix the rice, the water, the minced garlic, the soup and the broccoli.
4. Combine the mixture very well.
5. Remove the chicken from the Air fryer and place it on a platter to drain.
6. Spread the rice mixture on the bottom of the dish and place the chicken on top of the rice. Cook again for 30 minutes.

Asian-Style Chicken

(Prep + Cook Time: 35 minutes / Servings: 4)

Nutritional info per serving:

Calories 313, Carbohydrates 64 g, Fat 14 g, Protein 31 g

Ingredients:

1 lb. chicken, cut in stripes
2 tomatoes, cubed
3 green peppers, cut in stripes
1 tbsp. cumin powder
1 large onion

2 tbsp. oil
1 tbsp. mustard
1 pinch ginger
1 pinch fresh and chopped coriander
salt and black pepper

Directions:

1. Heat the oil in a deep pan. Add the mustard, the onion, the ginger, the cumin and the green chili peppers. Sauté the mixture for a 2-3 minutes.
2. Then add the tomatoes, the coriander and salt and keep stirring.
3. Preheat the Air Fryer to 380° F.
4. Coat the chicken with oil, salt and pepper and cook it for 25 minutes.
5. Remove it from the Air Fryer and pour the sauce over and around.

Crumbed Sage Chicken Scallopini

(Prep + Cook Time: 12 minutes / Servings: 4)

Nutritional info per serving:

Calories 218, Carbohydrates 8.9 g, Fat 5.9 g, Protein 30.4 g

Ingredients:

4 chicken breasts, skinless and boneless
3 oz. breadcrumbs
2 tbsp. grated Parmesan cheese
2 oz. flour

2 eggs, beaten
1 tbsp. fresh, chopped sage
Cooking spray

Directions:

1. Preheat the air fryer to 370 degrees F.
2. Place some plastic wrap underneath and on top of the chicken breasts.
3. Using a rolling pin beat the meat until it becomes really thin.
4. In a small bowl, combine the Parmesan, sage and breadcrumbs.
5. Dip the chicken in the egg first, and then in the sage mixture.
6. Spray with cooking oil and arrange the meat in the air fryer. Cook for about 7 minutes.

Buttermilk Chicken Thighs

(Prep + Cook Time: 4 hours 40 minutes / Servings: 6)

Nutritional info per serving:

Calories 322, Carbohydrates 36.3 g, Fat 4.2 g, Protein 32.7 g

Ingredients:

1 ½ lb. chicken thighs
1 tsp. cayenne pepper
3 tsp. salt divided
2 cups flour

2 tsp. black pepper
1 tbsp. paprika
1 tbsp. baking powder
2 cups buttermilk

Directions:

1. Rinse and pat dry the chicken thighs.
2. Place the chicken thighs in a bowl.
3. Add cayenne pepper, 2 tsp. salt, black pepper and buttermilk, and stir to coat well.
4. Refrigerate for 4 hours.
5. Preheat the air fryer to 350 degrees F.
6. In another bowl, mix the flour, paprika, 1 tsp. salt, and baking powder.
7. Dredge half of the chicken thighs, one at a time, in the flour, and then place on a lined dish.
8. Cook for 10 minutes, flip them over and cook for 8 more minutes.
9. Repeat with the other batch.

Sweet Garlicky Chicken Wings

(Prep + Cook Time: 20 minutes / Servings: 4)

Nutritional info per serving:

Calories 335, Carbohydrates 22 g, Fat 24 g, Protein 30 g

Ingredients:

16 chicken wings

¼ cup butter

¼ cup honey

½ tsp. salt

4 garlic cloves, minced

¾ cup potato starch

Directions:

1. Preheat the air fryer to 370 degrees F.

2. Rinse and pat dry the wings, and place them in a bowl.

3. Add the starch to the bowl, and mix to coat the chicken.

4. Place the chicken in a baking dish that has been previously coated slightly with cooking oil. Cook for 5 minutes. Meanwhile, whisk the rest of the ingredients together in a bowl.

5. Pour the sauce over the wings and cook for another 10 minutes.

Korean-Style Barbecued Satay

(Prep + Cook Time: 4h 15 minutes / Servings: 4)

Nutritional info per serving:

Calories 215, Carbohydrates 15 g, Fat 8 g, Protein 27 g

Ingredients:

1 lb. boneless and skinless chicken tenders

4 cloves garlic, chopped

4 scallions, chopped

2 tsp. sesame seeds, toasted

1 tsp. fresh ginger, grated

½ cup pineapple juice

½ cup soy sauce

⅓ cup sesame oil

1 pinch black pepper

Directions:

1. Skew each tender and trim any excess fat.
2. Mix the other ingredients in one large bowl.
3. Add the skewered chicken and place in the fridge for 4 to 24 hours.
4. Preheat the Air Fryer to 375°F.
5. Using paper towel, pat the chicken until it is completely dry.
6. Fry for 10 minutes.

Spicy Chicken Wings

(Prep + Cook Time: 25 minutes / Servings: 2)

Nutritional info per serving:

Calories 273, Carbohydrates 19 g, Fat 12 g, Protein 25 g

Ingredients:

10 chicken wings
2 tbsp. hot chili sauce
½ tbsp. lime juice

½ tbsp. honey
½ tsp kosher salt
½ tsp black pepper

Directions:

1. Preheat the Air Fryer to 350° F.
2. Mix the lime juice, honey and chili sauce.
3. Toss the mixture over the chicken wings.
4. Put the chicken wings in the Air Fryer basket and cook for 25 minutes.
5. Shake the basket every 5 minutes.

Thyme Turkey Nuggets

(Prep + Cook Time: 20 minutes / Servings: 2)

Nutritional info per serving:

Calories 423, Carbohydrates 50.9, Fat 8.6 g, Protein 34 g

Ingredients:

8 oz. turkey breast, boneless and skinless

1 egg, beaten

1 cup breadcrumbs

1 tbsp. dried thyme

½ tsp. dried parsley

Salt and pepper, to taste

Directions:

1. Preheat the air fryer to 350 degrees F.
2. Mince the turkey in a food processor. Transfer to a bowl.
3. Stir in the thyme and parsley, and season with salt and pepper.
4. Take a nugget-sized piece of the turkey mixture and shape it into a ball, or another form.
5. Dip it in the breadcrumbs, then egg, then in the breadcrumbs again.
6. Place the nuggets onto a prepared baking dish.
7. Air fry for 10 minutes.
8. Enjoy.

Thai Roasted Beef

(Prep + Cook Time: 4 hours 20 minutes / Servings: 2)

Nutritional info per serving:

Calories 700, Carbohydrates 21 g, Fat 39 g, Protein 64 g

Ingredients:

1 lb. round beef
½ tsp. salt
2 tbsp. soy sauce
½ tsp. pepper
Thumb-sized piece of ginger, chopped
3 chilies, deseeded and chopped
4 garlic cloves, chopped

1 tsp. brown sugar
Juice of 1 lime
2 tbsp. mirin
2 tbsp. coriander, chopped
2 tbsp. basil, chopped
2 tbsp. oil
2 tbsp. fish sauce

Directions:

1. Place all of the ingredients, except the beef, salt and pepper, in a blender.
2. Process until smooth.
3. Season the beef with salt and pepper.
4. Pace the beef and the Thai mixture in a zipper bag.
5. Shake well to combine and leave it to marinade in the fridge for about 4 hours.
6. Preheat the air fryer to 350 degrees.
7. Place the beef in the air fryer and cook for about 12 minutes, or more if you like it really well done.
8. Let sit for a couple of minutes before serving.

Peppercorn Meatloaf

(Prep + Cook Time: 35 minutes / Servings: 8)

Nutritional info per serving:

Calories 613, Carbohydrates 18 g, Fat 27 g, Protein 41 g

Ingredients:

4 lb. ground beef
1 tbsp. basil
1 tbsp. oregano
1 tbsp. parsley
1 onion, diced
1 tbsp. Worcestershire sauce

3 tbsp. ketchup
½ tsp. salt
1 tsp. ground peppercorns
10 whole peppercorns, for garnishing
1 cup breadcrumbs

Directions:

1. Preheat the air fryer to 350 degrees F.
2. Place the beef in a large bowl.
3. Add all of the ingredients except the whole peppercorns and the breadcrumbs.
4. Mix with your hand until well combined.
5. Stir in the breadcrumbs.
6. Place the meatloaf on a lined baking dish.
7. Place in the air fryer and cook for 25 minutes.
8. Garnish the meatloaf with the whole peppercorns and let cool slightly before serving.
9. Enjoy.

Apple and Onion Topped Pork Chops

(Prep + Cook Time: 25 minutes / Servings: 3)

Nutritional info per serving:

Calories 434, Carbohydrates 30 g, Fat 33 g, Protein 27 g

Ingredients:

Topping:

1 small onion, sliced
2 tbsp. olive oil
1 tbsp. apple cider vinegar
2 tsp. thyme

¼ tsp. brown sugar
1 cup sliced apples
2 tsp. rosemary

Meat:

¼ tsp. smoked paprika
1 tbsp. olive oil
3 pork chops

1 tbsp. apple cider vinegar
Salt and pepper, to taste

Directions:

1. Preheat the air fryer to 350 degrees F.
2. Place all of the topping ingredients in a baking dish and then in the air fryer.
3. Cook for about 4 minutes. Meanwhile, place the pork chops in a bowl.
4. Add olive oil, vinegar, paprika, and season with some salt and pepper.
5. Stir to coat them well.
6. Remove the topping from the dish.
7. Add the pork chops in the dish and cook in the air fryer for 10 minutes.
8. Place the topping on top, return to the air fryer and cook for 5 more minutes.
9. Enjoy.

Honey Barbecue Pork Ribs

(Prep + Cook Time: 4 h 35 minutes / Servings: 2)

Nutritional info per serving:

Calories 940, Carbohydrates 22 g, Fat 69 g, Protein 55 g

Ingredients:

1 lb. pork ribs
½ tsp. five spice powder
1 tsp. salt
3 garlic cloves, chopped
1 tsp. black pepper

1 tsp. sesame oil
1 tbsp. honey, plus some more for brushing
4 tbsp. barbecue sauce
1 tsp. soy sauce

Directions:

1. Chop the ribs into smaller pieces and place them in a large bowl. In a smaller bowl, whisk together all of the other ingredients. Add them to the bowl with the pork, and mix until the pork is fully coated.

2. Cover the bowl, place it in the fridge, and let it marinate for about 4 hours.

3. Preheat the air fryer to 350 degrees F. Place the ribs in the basket of the air fryer. Cook for 15 minutes. Brush the ribs with some honey and cook for another 15 minutes.

The Crispiest Roast Pork

(Prep + Cook Time: 3 hours 10 minutes / Servings: 4)

Nutritional info per serving:

Calories 940, Carbohydrates 22 g, Fat 69 g, Protein 55 g

Ingredients:

1 ½ lb. pork belly, blanched (cooked in boiling water for 2 to 4 minutes)
1 tsp. five spice seasoning

½ tsp. white pepper
¾ tsp. garlic powder
1 tsp. salt

Directions:

1. After blanching the pork belly leave it at room temperature for 2 hours to air dry. Pat with some paper towels if there is excess water. Preheat the air fryer to 330 degrees.
2. Take a skewer and pierce the skin as many times as you can, so you can ensure crispiness. Combine the seasonings in a small bowl, and rub it onto the pork.
3. Place the pork into the air fryer and cook for 30 minutes. Increase the temperature to 350 degrees F and cook for 30 more minutes.
4. Let cool slightly before serving.

Pork Belly the Philippine Style

(Prep + Cook Time: 4 hours 50 minutes / Servings: 6)

Nutritional info per serving:

Calories 800, Carbohydrates 1.2 g, Fat 82 g, Protein 14 g

Ingredients:

2 lb. pork belly, cut in half, blanched (cooked in boiling water for 2 to 4 minutes)

2 bay leaves	1 tbsp. peppercorns
2 tbsp. soy sauce	1 tbsp. peanut oil
5 garlic cloves, coarsely chopped	1 tsp. salt

Directions:

1. Let the blanched pork air dry for 2 hours. Pat the excess water if any.
2. Take a mortar and pestle and place bay leaves, garlic, salt, peppercorns, and peanut oil in it. Smash until a paste-like consistency has formed.
3. Whisk the paste with the soy sauce.
4. Pierce the skin of the pork belly with a fork or a skewer. Rub the mixture onto the meat. Wrap the pork with a plastic foil and refrigerate for 2 hours.
5. Preheat the air fryer to 350 degrees F. Place the pork in the basket of the air fryer and cook for 30 minutes. Increase the temperature to 370 degrees F and cook for 10 more.

Char Siew Pork Ribs

(Prep + Cook Time: 55 minutes / Servings: 6)

Nutritional info per serving:

Calories 753, Carbohydrates 15 g, Fat 37 g, Protein 33g

Ingredients:

2 lb. pork ribs

2 tbsp. char siew sauce

2 tbsp. minced ginger

2 tbsp. hoisin sauce

2 tbsp. sesame oil

1 tbsp. honey

4 garlic cloves, minced

1 tbsp. soy sauce

Directions:

1. Whisk together all of the marinate ingredients in a small bowl.

2. Coat the ribs well with the mixture. Place in a container with a lid, and refrigerate for 4 hours. Preheat the air fryer to 330 degrees F.

3. Place the ribs in the basket but do not throw away the liquid from the container.

4. Cook for 40 minutes.

5. Stir in the liquid, increase the temperature to 350 degrees, and cook 10 more minutes.

Crunchy Cashew Lamb Rack

(Prep + Cook Time: 30 minutes / Servings: 4)

Nutritional info per serving:

Calories 262 Carbohydrates 1.5 g, Fat 11.8 g, Protein 35 g

Ingredients:

3 oz. chopped cashews

1 tbsp. chopped rosemary

1 ½ lb. rack of lamb

1 garlic clove, minced

1 tbsp. breadcrumbs

1 egg, beaten

1 tbsp. olive oil salt and pepper, to taste

Directions:

1. Preheat the air fryer to 210 degrees F.
2. Combine the o
3. live oil with the garlic and brush this mixture onto the lamb.
4. Meanwhile, combine the rosemary, cashews, and breadcrumbs, in a small bowl.
5. Brush the egg over the lambs, and then coat it with the cashew mixture.
6. Place the lamb into the basket of the air fryer and cook for 25 minutes.
7. Increase the temperature to 390 degrees F, and cook for additional 5 minutes.
8. Cover with a foil and let sit for a couple of minutes before serving.

Oregano and Thyme Lamb Chops

(Prep + Cook Time: 30 minutes / Servings: 4)

Nutritional info per serving:

Calories 270, Carbohydrates 0.2g, Fat 13 g, Protein 34.8 g

Ingredients:

4 lamb chops
1 garlic clove, peeled
1 tbsp. plus
2 tsp. olive oil

½ tbsp. oregano
½ tbsp. thyme
½ tsp. salt
¼ tsp. black pepper

Directions:

1. Preheat the air fryer to 390 degrees F.
2. Coat the garlic clove with 1 tsp. of olive oil and place it in the air fryer for 10 minutes.
3. Meanwhile, mix the herbs and seasonings with the remaining olive oil.
4. Using a towel or a mitten, squeeze the hot roasted garlic clove into the herb mixture and stir to combine.
5. Coat the lamb chops with the mixture well, and place in the air fryer.
6. Cook for about 8 to 12 minutes.

Lamb Meatballs

(Prep + Cook Time: 40 minutes / Servings: 12)

Nutritional info per serving:

Calories 304, Carbohydrates 1.3 g, Fat 16 g, Protein 21 g

Ingredients:

1 ½ lb. ground lamb
½ cup minced onion
2 tbsp. chopped mint leaves
3 garlic cloves, minced
2 tsp. paprika
2 tsp. coriander seeds

½ tsp. cayenne pepper
1 tsp. salt
1 tbsp. chopped parsley
2 tsp. cumin
½ tsp. ground ginger

Directions:

1. Soak 24 skewers in water, until ready to use.
2. Preheat the air fryer to 330 degrees F.
3. Combine all of the ingredients in a large bowl.
4. Make sure to mix well with your hands until the herbs and spices are evenly distributed and the mixture is well incorporated.
5. Shape the lamb mixture into 12 sausage shapes around 2 skewers.
6. Cook for about 12 to 15 minutes, or until it reaches the preferred doneness.
7. Served as desired (I suggest tzatziki sauce) and enjoy.

Pasta with Roasted Veggies

(Prep + Cook Time: 25 minutes / Servings: 6)

Nutritional info per serving:

Calories 391, Carbohydrates 64.4 g, Fat 14.4 g, Protein 9.5 g

Ingredients:

1 lb. penne, cooked

1 zucchini, sliced

1 pepper, sliced

1 acorn squash, sliced

4 oz. mushrooms, sliced

½ cup kalamata olives, pitted and halved

¼ cup olive oil

1 tsp. Italian seasoning

1 cup grape tomatoes, halved

3 tbsp. balsamic vinegar

2 tbsp. chopped basil

Salt and pepper, to taste

Directions:

1. Preheat the air fryer to 380 degrees F.
2. Combine the pepper, zucchini, squash, mushrooms, and olive oil, in a large bowl.
3. Season with some salt and pepper.
4. Air fry the veggies for 15 minutes.
5. In a large bowl, combine the penne, roasted vegetables, olives, tomatoes, Italian seasoning, and vinegar.
6. Sprinkle basil and serve.

Poblano and Tomato Stuffed Squash

(Prep + Cook Time: 50 minutes / Servings: 3)

Nutritional info per serving:

Calories 98, Carbohydrates 8.2 g, Fat 5.3 g, Protein 4.3 g

Ingredients:

½ butternut squash
6 grape tomatoes, halved
1 poblano pepper, cut into strips

¼ cup grated mozzarella, optional
2 tsp. olive oil divided
Salt and pepper, to taste

Directions:

1. Preheat the air fryer to 350 degrees F. Meanwhile, cut trim the ends and cut the squash lengthwise. You will only need one half for this recipe.
2. Scoop the flash out, so you make room for the filling.
3. Brush 1 tsp. oil over the squash. Place in the air fryer and roast for 30 minutes.
4. Combine the other teaspoon of olive oil with the tomatoes and poblanos.
5. Season with salt and pepper, to taste. Place the peppers and tomatoes into the squash. Cook for 15 more minutes.
6. If using mozzarella, add it on top of the squash, two minutes before the end.

Spicy Pepper, Sweet Potato Skewers

(Prep + Cook Time: 20 minutes / Servings: 1)

Nutritional info per serving:

Calories 335, Carbohydrates 49.6 g, Fat 14.3 g, Protein 4.9 g

Ingredients:

1 large sweet potato
1 beetroot
1 green bell pepper
1 tsp. chili flakes
¼ tsp. black pepper

½ tsp. turmeric
¼ tsp. garlic powder
¼ tsp. paprika
1 tbsp. olive oil

Directions:

1. Soak 3 to 4 skewers until ready to use. Preheat the air fryer to 350 degrees F.
2. Peel the veggies and cut them into bite-sized chunks.
3. Place the chunks in a bowl along with the remaining ingredients. Mix until fully coated.
4. Thread the veggies in this order: potato, pepper, beetroot.
5. Place in the air fryer and cook for 15 minutes.
6. Enjoy.

Grilled Tofu Sandwich

(Prep + Cook Time: 20 minutes / Servings: 1)

Nutritional info per serving:

Calories 225.8, Carbohydrates 21.5 g, Fat 30.5 g, Protein 12.3g

Ingredients:

2 slices of bread
1 1-inch thick Tofu slice
¼ cup red cabbage, shredded

2 tsp. olive oil divided
¼ tsp. vinegar
Salt and pepper, to taste

Directions:

1. Preheat the air fryer to 350 degrees F.
2. Place the bread slices and toast for 3 minutes.
3. Set aside.
4. Brush the tofu with 1 tsp. oil and place in the basket of the air fryer.
5. Grill for 5 minutes on each side.
6. Combine the cabbage, remaining oil, and vinegar, and season with salt and pepper.
7. Place the tofu on top of one bread slice, place the cabbage over, and top with the other bread slice.
8. Enjoy.

Quinoa and Veggie Stuffed Peppers

(Prep + Cook Time: 16 minutes / Servings: 1)

Nutritional info per serving:

Calories 190, Carbohydrates 29.6 g, Fat 6.6 g, Protein 5.7 g

Ingredients:

¼ cup cooked quinoa

1 bell pepper

½ tbsp. diced onion

½ diced tomato, plus one tomato slice

¼ tsp. smoked paprika

Salt and pepper, to taste

1 tsp. olive oil

¼ tsp. dried basil

Directions:

1. Preheat the air fryer to 350 degrees F. Core and clean the bell pepper to prepare it for stuffing. Brush the pepper with half of the olive oil on the outside.

2. In a small bowl, combine all of the other ingredients, except the tomato slice and reserved half-teaspoon olive oil.

3. Stuff the pepper with the filling. Top with the tomato slice.

4. Brush the tomato slice with the remaining half-teaspoon of olive oil and sprinkle with basil. Air fry for 10 minutes.

Tasty Baby Porcupine

(Prep + Cook Time: 30 minutes / Servings: 4)

Nutritional info per serving:

Calories 255, Carbohydrates 31 g, Fat 15.5 g, Protein 19.5 g

Ingredients:

⅓ cup of rice

2/2 lb. of ground beef

2/3 tbsp. of minced onion

2 tbsp. green bell peppers, finely chopped

1 tsp. celery salt

2 tbsp. of Worcestershire sauce

1 clove of garlic

2 cups of tomato juice

1 tsp. oregano

Directions:

1. Combine the rice and the ground beef, the onion, the celery salt, the green peppers and the garlic.
2. Shape into balls of 1 inch each.
3. Arrange the balls in the basket of the Air Fryer.
4. Cook for 25 minutes at 320° F and bake the balls.
5. Meanwhile, heat the tomato juice, the cloves, the oregano and the Worcestershire sauce.
6. Serve the balls with the sauce.

Avocado Rolls

(Prep + Cook Time: 15 minutes / Servings: 5)

Nutritional info per serving:

Calories 270, Carbohydrates 24.7 g, Fat 18.7 g, Protein 5.8g

Ingredients:

3 ripe avocados, pitted and peeled   ¼ tsp. pepper
10 egg roll wrappers   ½ tsp. salt
1 tomato, diced

Directions:

1. Place all of the filling ingredients in a bowl.
2. Mash with a fork until somewhat smooth. There should be chunks left.
3. Divide the feeling between the egg wrappers.
4. Wet your finger and brush along the edges, so the wrappers can seal well.
5. Roll and seal the wrappers.
6. Arrange them on a baking sheet lined dish, and place in the air fryer.
7. Air fry at 350 degrees F, for 5 minutes.
8. Serve with favorite dipping (I recommend a chili one) and enjoy.

Vegetable Tortilla Pizza

(Prep + Cook Time: 15 minutes / Servings: 1)

Nutritional info per serving:

Calories 385, Carbohydrates 50.2 g, Fat 12.4 g, Protein 21.7 g

Ingredients:

1 ½ tbsp. tomato paste
¼ cup grated cheddar cheese
¼ cup grated mozzarella cheese
1 tbsp. cooked sweet corn
4 zucchini slices
4 eggplant slices

4 red onion Rings
½ green bell pepper, chopped
3 cherry tomatoes, quartered
1 tortilla
¼ tsp. basil
¼ tsp. oregano

Directions:

1. Preheat the air fryer to 350 degrees F. Spread the tomato paste on the tortilla.

2. Arrange the zucchini and eggplant slices first, then green peppers, and onion rings.

3. Arrange the cherry tomatoes and sprinkle the sweet corn over.

4. Sprinkle with oregano and basil. Top with cheddar and mozzarella.

5. Place in the air fryer and cook for 10 minutes.

Paneer Cutlet

(Prep + Cook Time: 15 minutes / Servings: 1)

Nutritional info per serving:

Calories 567, Carbohydrates 21 g, Fat 23 g, Protein 19 g

Ingredients:

2 cup grated paneer
1 cup grated cheese
½ tsp. chai masala
1 tsp. butter

½ tsp. garlic powder
1 small onion, finely chopped
½ tsp. oregano
½ tsp. salt

Directions:

1. Preheat the air fryer to 350 degrees F.
2. Grease a baking dish.
3. Mix all of the ingredients in a bowl, until well incorporated.
4. Make cutlets out of the mixture and place them on the greased baking dish.
5. Place the baking dish in the air fryer and cook the cutlets for 10 minutes.
6. Enjoy.

Simple Air Fried Ravioli

(Prep + Cook Time: 15 minutes / Servings: 6)

Nutritional info per serving:

Calories 298.8, Carbohydrates 42.1 g, Fat 8.7 g, Protein 13.4 g

Ingredients:

1 package cheese ravioli
2 cup Italian breadcrumbs
¼ cup Parmesan cheese

1 cup buttermilk
1 tsp. olive oil
¼ tsp. garlic powder

Directions:

1. Preheat the air fryer to 390 degrees F.
2. In a small bowl, combine the breadcrumbs, Parmesan cheese, garlic powder, and olive oil.
3. Dip the ravioli in the buttermilk and then coat them with the breadcrumb mixture.
4. Line a baking sheet with parchment paper and arrange the ravioli on it.
5. Place in the air fryer and cook for 5 minutes.
6. Serve the air-fried ravioli with favorite sauce (I used simple marinara jar sauce).
7. Enjoy.

Crispy Nachos

(Prep + Cook Time: 20 minutes / Servings: 2)

Nutritional info per serving:

Calories 251, Carbohydrates 25 g, Fat 11.4 g, Protein 8 g

Ingredients:

1 cup sweet corn	½ tsp. chili powder
1 cup all-purpose flour	2-3 tbsp. water
1 tbsp. butter	salt

Directions:

1. Add a small amount of water to the sweet corn and grind until you obtain a very fine paste. In a large bowl, add the flour, the salt, the chili powder, the butter and mix very well. Add the corn and stir well.

2. Start to knead with your palm until you obtain a stiff dough. Preheat the air fryer to 350° F. Meanwhile, dust a little bit of flour and spread the dough with a rolling pin.

3. Make it around ½ inch thick. Cut it in any shape you want and fry the shapes in the Air Fryer for around 10 minutes. Serve with guacamole salsa.

Veggie Skewers

(Prep + Cook Time: 20 minutes / Servings: 4)

Nutritional info per serving:

Calories 211, Carbohydrates 25 g, Fat 11.4 g, Protein 8 g

Ingredients:

2 tbsp. corn flour	½ cup paneer
2/3 cup canned beans	1 green chili
⅓ cup grated carrots	1-inch piece of fresh ginger
2 boiled and mashed potatoes	3 garlic cloves
¼ cup chopped fresh mint leaves	Salt, to taste
½ tsp. garam masala powder	

Directions:

1. Soak 12 skewers until ready to use.
2. Preheat the air fryer to 390 degrees F.
3. Place the beans, carrots, garlic, ginger, chili, paneer, and mint, in a food processor and process until smooth. Transfer to a bowl.
4. Add the mashed potatoes, corn flour, some salt, and garam masala powder to the bowl.
5. Mix until fully incorporate.
6. Divide the mixture into 12 equal pieces. (Mine were lemon-sized.)
7. Shape each of the pieces around a skewer.
8. Air fry the skewers for 10 minutes.

Quick Crispy Kale Chips

(Prep + Cook Time: 9 minutes / Servings: 2)

Nutritional info per serving:

Calories 107, Carbohydrates 18 g, Fat 18.4 g, Protein 5.2 g

Ingredients:

4 cups kale, stemmed and packed
2 tbsp. of olive oil
1 tbsp. of yeast flakes

1 tsp. of vegan seasoning
salt

Directions:

1. In a bowl, add the oil, the kale, the vegan seasoning, and the yeast and mix well.
2. Dump the coated kale in the Air Fryer's basket.
3. Set the heat to 370° F and fry for a total of 6 minutes
4. Shake it from time to time.

Paneer Cheese Balls

(Prep + Cook Time: 12 minutes / Servings: 2)

Nutritional info per serving:

Calories 257, Carbohydrates 31 g, Fat 22 g, Protein 16 g

Ingredients:

2 oz. paneer cheese

2 tbsp. flour

2 medium onions, chopped

1 tbsp. corn flour

1 green chili, chopped

1-inch ginger piece, chopped

1 tsp. red chili powder

a few leaves of coriander, chopped

oil and salt

Directions:

1. Mix all ingredients, except the oil and the cheese.
2. Take a small part of the mixture, roll it up and slowly press it to flatten it.
3. Stuff in 1 cube of cheese and seal the edges. Repeat with the rest of the mixture.
4. Fry the balls in the Air Fryer for 12 minutes and at 370° F.
5. Serve hot with ketchup!

Potato Filled Bread Rolls

(Prep + Cook Time: 25 minutes / Servings: 4)

Nutritional info per serving:

Calories 451, Carbohydrates 93.5 g, Fat 5.2 g, Protein 14.2 g

Ingredients:

8 slices of bread

5 large potatoes, boiled and mashed

½ tsp. turmeric

2 green chilies, deseeded and chopped

1 medium onion, finely chopped

½ tsp. mustard seeds

1 tbsp. olive oil

2 sprigs curry leaf

Salt, to taste

Directions:

1. Preheat the air fryer to 350 degrees F.
2. Combine the olive oil, onion, curry leaves, and mustard seed, in a baking dish. Air fry for 5 minutes.
3. Mix the onion mixture with the mashed potatoes, chilies, turmeric, and some salt. Divide the mixture into 8 equal pieces.
4. Trim the sides of the bread, and wet it with some water.
5. Make sure to get rid of the excess water.
6. Take one wet bread slice in your palm and pace one of the potato pieces in the center.
7. Roll the bread over the filling, sealing the edges.
8. Place the rolls onto a prepared baking dish, and air fry for 12 minutes.

Quick Crispy Cheese Lings

(Prep + Cook Time: 15 minutes / Servings: 4)

Nutritional info per serving:

Calories 155, Carbohydrates 23.5 g, Fat 17.3 g, Protein 11.6 g

Ingredients:

4 cups of grated cheese, any
1 cup of all-purpose flour
1 tbsp. of butter
1 tbsp. of baking powder

¼ tsp. of chili powder
¼ tsp. salt, to taste
1-2 tbsp. water

Directions:

1. Mix the flour and the baking powder. Add the chili powder, salt, butter, cheese and 1-2 tbsp. of water to the mixture.
2. Make a stiff dough. Knead the dough for a while. Sprinkle a tbsp. or so of flour on the table. Tale a rolling pin and roll the dough into ½ -inch thickness.
3. Cut the dough in any shape you want and fry the cheese lings for 6 minutes at 370° F.

Prawn Toast

(Prep + Cook Time: 12 minutes / Servings: 2)

Nutritional info per serving:

Calories 158, Carbohydrates 21 g, Fat14 g, Protein 25 g

Ingredients:

6 large prawns, shells removed
1 large spring onion, finely sliced
3 white slices of bread

½ cup sweet corn
1 egg white, whisked
1 tbsp. black sesame seeds

Directions:

1. In a bowl, place the chopped prawns, corn, spring onion and the black sesame seeds.
2. Add the whisked egg and mix the ingredients..
3. Spread the mixture over the bread slices.
4. Place in the prawns in the Air Fryer's basket and sprinkle oil.
5. Fry the prawns until golden, for 8-10 minutes at 370° F.
6. Serve with ketchup or chili sauce.

Roasted Vegetable Salad

(Prep + Cook Time: 25 minutes / Servings: 1)

Nutritional info per serving:

Calories 263.8, Carbohydrates 21.4 g, Fat 12 g, Protein 10.7 g

Ingredients:

1 potato, peeled and chopped
¼ onion, sliced
1 carrot, sliced diagonally
½ small beetroot, sliced
1 cup cherry tomatoes
Juice of 1 lemon
Handful of rocket salad

Handful of baby spinach
3 tbsp. canned chickpeas
½ tsp. cumin
½ tsp. turmeric
¼ tsp. sea salt
2 tbsp. olive oil
Parmesan shavings

Directions:

1. Preheat the air fryer to 370 degrees F.
2. Combine the onion, potato, cherry tomatoes, carrot, beetroot, cumin, seas salt, turmeric, and 1 tbsp. olive oil, in a bowl.
3. Place in the air fryer and cook for 20 minutes.
4. Let cool for 2 minutes.
5. Place the rocket, salad, spinach, lemon juice, and 1 tbsp. olive oil, into a serving bowl.
6. Mix to combine.
7. Stir in the roasted veggies.
8. Top with chickpeas and Parmesan shavings.
9. Enjoy.

Pineapple Appetizer Ribs

(Prep + Cook Time: 30 minutes / Servings: 4)

Nutritional info per serving:

Calories 386, Carbohydrates 54.7 g, Fat 17.5 g, Protein 32.7 g

Ingredients:

2 lb. cut spareribs

7 oz. salad dressing

5 oz. can pineapple juice

2 cups water

garlic salt

salt and black pepper

Directions:

1. Sprinkle the ribs with salt and pepper and place them in a saucepan.
2. Pour water and cook the ribs for around 12 minutes on high heat.
3. Drain the ribs and arrange them in the Air Fryer.
4. Sprinkle with garlic salt.
5. Cook for 15 minutes at 390° F.
6. Meanwhile, prepare the sauce by combining the salad dressing and the pineapple juice.
7. Serve the ribs with this delicious dressing sauce!

Crispy Ham Rolls

(Prep + Cook Time: 17 minutes / Servings: 3)

Nutritional info per serving:

Calories 246, Carbohydrates 41.7 g, Fat 21.5 g, Protein 18.7 g

Ingredients:

1 lb. chopped ham

3 packages Pepperidge farm rolls

1 tbsp. softened butter

1 tsp. mustard seeds

1 tsp. poppy seeds

1 small chopped onion

Directions:

1. Mix the butter, the mustard, the onion and the poppy seeds.
2. Spread the mixture on top of the rolls.
3. Cover the bottom halves with the chopped ham.
4. Arrange the rolls in the basket of the Air Fryer.
5. Cook on 350° F for about 15 minutes.
6. Enjoy.

Fish and Seafood Recipes

Parmesan Tilapia

(Prep + Cook Time: 15 minutes / Servings: 4)

Nutritional info per serving:

Calories 228.4, Carbohydrates 1.3 g, Fat 11.1 g, Protein 31.9 g

Ingredients:

¾ cup grated Parmesan cheese
1 tbsp. olive oil
2 tsp. paprika
1 tbsp. chopped parsley

¼ tsp. garlic powder
¼ tsp. salt
4 tilapia fillets

Directions:

1. Preheat the air fryer to 350 degrees F.
2. Mix parsley, Parmesan, garlic, salt, and paprika in a shallow bowl.
3. Brush the olive oil over the fillets, and then coat them with the Parmesan mixture.
4. Place the tilapia onto a lined baking sheet, and then into the air fryer.
5. Cook for about 4 to 5 minutes on all sides.

Fish Finger Sandwich

(Prep + Cook Time: 20 minutes / Servings: 4)

Nutritional info per serving:

Calories 360.7, Carbohydrates 39.2 g, Fat 10.4 g, Protein 29.3 g

Ingredients:

4 cod fillets
2 tbsp. flour

10 capers
4 bread rolls

2 oz. breadcrumbs

4 tbsp. pesto sauce

4 lettuce leaves

Salt and pepper, to taste

Directions:

1. Preheat the air fryer to 370 degrees F.
2. Season the fillets with some salt and pepper, and coat them with the flour, and then dip in the breadcrumbs. You should get a really thin layer of breadcrumbs, that's why we don't use eggs for this recipe.
3. Arrange the fillets onto a baking mat.
4. Air fry for about 10 to 15 minutes. Cut the bread rolls in half.
5. Place a lettuce leaf on top of the bottom halves. Place the fillets over.
6. Spread a tablespoon of pesto sauce on top of each fillet. Top with the remaining halves.

Quick and Easy Air Fried Salmon

(Prep + Cook Time: 13 minutes / Servings: 1)

Nutritional info per serving:

Calories 172, Carbohydrates 1.7 g, Fat 7.2 g, Protein 23.7 g

Ingredients:

1 salmon fillet

1 tbsp. soy sauce

¼ tsp. garlic powder

Salt and pepper

Directions:

1. Preheat the air fryer to 350 degrees F.
2. Combine the soy sauce with the garlic powder and some salt and pepper.
3. Brush the mixture over the salmon.
4. Place the salmon onto a sheet of parchment paper and into the air fryer.
5. Cook for 10 minutes.
6. Enjoy.

Delicious Coconut Shrimp

(Prep + Cook Time: 30 minutes / Servings: 2)

Nutritional info per serving:

Calories 436, Carbohydrates 69.9 g, Fat 16.4 g, Protein 7.6 g

Ingredients:

8 large shrimp
½ cup breadcrumbs
8 oz. coconut milk
½ cup shredded coconut
¼ tsp. salt
¼ tsp. pepper

½ cup orange jam
1 tsp. mustard
1 tbsp. honey
½ tsp. cayenne pepper
¼ tsp. hot sauce

Directions:

1. Preheat the air fryer to 350 degrees F.
2. Combine the breadcrumbs, cayenne pepper, shredded coconut, salt, and pepper in a small bowl.
3. Dip the shrimp in the coconut milk, first, and then in the coconut crumbs.
4. Arrange on a lined sheet, and air fry for 20 minutes.
5. Meanwhile whisk the jam, honey, hot sauce, and mustard.
6. Serve the shrimp with the sauce.
7. Enjoy.

Crab Cakes

(Prep + Cook Time: 55 minutes / Servings: 4)

Nutritional info per serving:

Calories 159.6, Carbohydrates 5.1 g, Fat 10.4 g, Protein 11.3 g

Ingredients:

½ cup cooked crab meat
¼ cup chopped red onion
1 tbsp. chopped basil
¼ cup chopped celery
¼ cup chopped red pepper
3 tbsp. mayonnaise

Zest of half a lemon
¼ cup breadcrumbs
2 tbsp. chopped parsley
Old Bay seasoning, as desired
Cooking spray

Directions:

1. Preheat the air fryer to 390 degrees F. Place all of the ingredients in a large bowl and mix well until completely incorporated.

2. Make 4 large crab cakes from the mixture and place them on a lined sheet.

3. Refrigerate for about 30 minutes, to set.

4. Spay the air basket with cooking spray and arrange the crab cakes in it.

5. Cook for about 7 minutes on each side.

Cajun Salmon with Lemon

(Prep + Cook Time: 10 minutes / Servings: 1)

Nutritional info per serving:

Calories 170, Carbohydrates 9 g, Fat 7.2 g, Protein 22.6 g

Ingredients:

1 salmon fillet
¼ tsp. brown sugar
Juice of ½ lemon

1 tbsp. Cajun seasoning
2 lemon wedges
1 tbsp. chopped parsley, for garnishing

Directions:

1. Preheat the air fryer to 350 degrees F.
2. Meanwhile, Combine the sugar and lemon and coat the salmon with this mixture completely.
3. Coat the salmon with the Cajun seasoning as well.
4. Place a parchment paper into the air fryer and cook the salmon for 7 minutes. Remember if using a thicker fillet, cook no more than 6 minutes.
5. Serve with lemon wedges and chopped parsley.
6. Enjoy.

Cod Cornflakes Nuggets

(Prep + Cook Time: 25 minutes / Servings: 4)

Nutritional info per serving:

Calories 267.7, Carbohydrates 15.9 g, Fat 5.8 g, Protein 35.1 g

Ingredients:

1 ¼ lb. cod fillets, cut into 4 to 6 chunks each
½ cup flour
1 egg
1 tbsp. water
1 cup (use more if needed) cornflakes
1 tbsp. olive oil salt and pepper, to taste

Directions:

1. Place the oil and cornflakes in a food processor and process until crumbed.
2. Season the fish chunks with some salt and pepper.
3. Beat the egg along with 1 tbsp. water.
4. Dredge the chunks in flour first, then dip in the egg, and coat with cornflakes.
5. Arrange on a lined sheet.
6. Air fry at 350 degrees for about 15 minutes.
7. Enjoy.

Tuna Patties

(Prep + Cook Time: 50 minutes / Servings: 2)

Nutritional info per serving:

Calories 235.5, Carbohydrates 20.5 g, Fat 6.6 g, Protein 24.6 g

Ingredients:

5 oz. of canned tuna
1 tsp. lime juice
1 tsp. paprika
¼ cup flour
½ cup milk

1 small onion, diced
2 eggs
1 tsp. chili powder, optional
½ tsp. salt

Directions:

1. Place all of the ingredients in a bowl and mix well to combine.

2. Make two large patties, or a few smaller ones, out of the mixture.

3. Place them on a lined sheet and refrigerate for 30 minutes.

4. Preheat the air fryer to 350 degrees F.

5. Air fry the patties for about 6 minutes on each side.

6. Enjoy.

Pistachio Crusted Salmon

(Prep + Cook Time: 15 minutes / Servings: 1)

Nutritional info per serving:

Calories 357, Carbohydrates 8.2 g, Fat 23.8 g, Protein 28.8 g

Ingredients:

1 salmon fillet
1 tsp. mustard
3 tbsp. pistachios

Pinch of sea salt
Pinch of garlic powder
Pinch of black pepper

1 tsp. lemon juice   1 tsp. olive oil

1 tsp. grated Parmesan cheese

Directions:

1. Preheat the air fryer to 350 degrees F.
2. Whisk the mustard and lemon juice together.
3. Season the salmon with salt, pepper, and garlic powder.
4. Brush the olive oil on all sides.
5. Brush the mustard/lemon mixture on top of the salmon.
6. Chop the pistachios finely and combine them with the Parmesan cheese.
7. Sprinkle them on top of the salmon.
8. Place the salmon in the air fryer basket with the skin side down.
9. Cook for about 10 minutes, or to your liking.

The Most Chocolaty Fudge

(Prep + Cook Time: 55 minutes / Servings: 8)

Nutritional info per serving:

Calories 494, Carbohydrates 65.7 g, Fat 25.1 g, Protein 5.6 g

Ingredients:

1 cup sugar

7 oz. flour

1 tbsp. honey

¼ cup milk

1 tsp. vanilla extract

1 oz. cocoa powder

2 eggs

4 oz. butter

1 orange, juice and zest

Icing:

1 oz. butter, melted

4 oz. powdered sugar

1 tbsp. brown sugar

1 tbsp. milk

2 tsp. honey

Directions:

1. Preheat the air fryer to 350 degrees F. In one bowl, mix the dry ingredients for the fudge.
2. Mix the wet ingredients separately.
3. Combine the two mixtures gently.
4. Transfer the batter to a prepared cake pan.
5. Bake for about 35 minutes.
6. Meanwhile whisk together all of the icing ingredients.
7. When the cake is cooled, coat it with the icing.
8. Let set before slicing the fudge.

White Chocolate Chip Cookies

(Prep + Cook Time: 30 minutes / Servings: 8)

Nutritional info per serving:

Calories 167, Carbohydrates 21.3 g, Fat 11.3 g, Protein 0.7 g

Ingredients:

6 oz. self-rising flour
3 oz. brown sugar
2 oz. white chocolate chips

1 tbsp. honey
1 ½ tbsp. milk
4 oz. butter

Directions:

1. Preheat the air fryer to 350 degrees F.
2. Beat the butter and sugar until fluffy.
3. Beat in the honey, milk, and flour.
4. Gently fold in the chocolate chip cookies.
5. Drop spoonfuls of the mixture onto a prepared cookie sheet.
6. Cook for 18 minutes.
7. Enjoy.

No Flour Lime Muffins

(Prep + Cook Time: 30 minutes / Servings: 6)

Nutritional info per serving:

Calories 200.7, Carbohydrates 14.1 g, Fat 11 g, Protein 11.8 g

Ingredients:

2 eggs plus 1 yolk
Juice and zest of 2 limes
1 cup yogurt
¼ cup superfine sugar

8 oz. cream cheese
1 tsp. vanilla extract

Directions:

1. Preheat the air fryer to 330 degrees F.
2. With a spatula, gently combine the yogurt and cheese.
3. In another bowl, beat together the rest of the ingredients.
4. Gently fold the lime with the cheese mixture.
5. Divide the batter between 6 lined muffin tins.
6. Bake in the air fryer for 10 minutes.

White Filling Coconut and Oat Cookies

(Prep + Cook Time: 30 minutes / Servings: 4)

Nutritional info per serving:

Calories 477, Carbohydrates 73.8 g, Fat 16.8 g, Protein 7.4 g

Ingredients:

5 ½ oz. flour
1 tsp. vanilla extract
3 oz. sugar

½ cup oats
1 small egg, beaten
¼ cup coconut flakes

Filling:

1 oz. white chocolate, melted
2 oz. butter

4 oz. powdered sugar
1 tsp. vanilla extract

Directions:

1. Beat all of the cookie ingredients, with an electric mixer, except the flour.
2. When smooth, fold in the flour.
3. Drop spoonfuls of the batter onto a prepared cookie sheet.
4. Cook in the air fryer at 350 degrees F for about 18 minutes. Let cool.
5. Meanwhile, prepare the filling by beating all the ingredients together. Spread the filling on half of the cookies.
6. Top with the other halves to make cookie sandwiches.

Molten Lava Cake

(Prep + Cook Time: 20 minutes / Servings: 4)

Nutritional info per serving:

Calories 785, Carbohydrates 31.6 g, Fat 60.2 g, Protein 30.7 g

Ingredients:

3 ½ oz. butter, melted

3 ½ tbsp. sugar

1 ½ tbsp. self-rising flour

3 ½ oz. dark chocolate, melted

2 eggs

Directions:

1. Grease 4 ramekins with butter. Preheat the air fryer to 375 degrees F.
2. Beat the eggs and sugar until frothy.
3. Stir in the butter and chocolate.
4. Gently fold in the flour.
5. Divide the mixture between the ramekins and bake in the air fryer for 10 minutes.
6. Let cool for 2 minutes before turning the lava cakes upside down onto serving plates.
7. Enjoy.

Air Fried Doughnuts

(Prep + Cook Time: 25 minutes / Servings: 4)

Nutritional info per serving:

Calories 253, Carbohydrates 42.5 g, Fat 9.4 g, Protein 5.6 g

Ingredients:

8 oz. self-rising flour

1 tsp. baking powder

½ cup milk

2 ½ tbsp. butter

1 egg

2 oz. brown sugar

Directions:

1. Preheat the air fryer to 350 degrees F.
2. Beat the butter with the sugar, until smooth.
3. Beat in eggs, and milk.
4. In a bowl, combine the flour with the baking powder.
5. Gently fold the flour into the butter mixture.
6. Form donut shapes and cut off the center with cookie cutters.
7. Arrange on a lined baking sheet and cook in the air fryer for 15 minutes.
8. Serve with whipped cream or favoring icing.

Air Fried Snickerdoodle Poppers

(Prep + Cook Time: 30 minutes / Servings: 6)

Nutritional info per serving:

Calories 278.6, Carbohydrates 75.1 g, Fat 2.4 g, Protein 4 g

Ingredients:

1 box instant vanilla Jell-O
1 can of Pillsbury Grands Flaky Layers
Biscuits

1 ½ cups cinnamon sugar
Melted butter, for brushing

Directions:

1. Preheat the air fryer to 350 degrees F.
2. Unroll the flaky biscuits and cut them into fourths. Roll each ¼ into a ball.
3. Arrange the balls on a lined baking sheet, and cook in the air fryer for 7 minutes, or until golden.
4. Meanwhile, prepare the Jell-O following the package's instructions.
5. Using an injector, inject some of the vanilla pudding into each ball.
6. Brush the balls with melted butter and then coat them with cinnamon sugar.
7. Enjoy.

Pineapple Cake

(Prep + Cook Time: 50 minutes / Servings: 4)

Nutritional info per serving:

Calories 411, Carbohydrates 42 g, Fat 5.1 g, Protein 4 g

Ingredients:

2 oz. dark chocolate, grated

8 oz. self-rising flour

4 oz. butter

7 oz. pineapple chunks

½ cup pineapple juice

1 egg

2 tbsp. milk

½ cup sugar

Directions:

1. Preheat the air fryer to 390 degrees F.
2. Place the butter and flour into a bowl and rub the mixture with your fingers until crumbed.
3. Stir in the pineapple, sugar, chocolate, and juice.
4. Beat the eggs and milk separately, and then add them to the batter.
5. Transfer the batter to a previously prepared (greased or lined) cake pan, and cook for 40 minutes. Let cool for at least 10 minutes before serving.

Chocolate Soufflé

(Prep + Cook Time: 25 minutes / Servings: 2)

Nutritional info per serving:

Calories 598, Carbohydrates 50.9 g, Fat 41.3 g, Protein 10.3 g

Ingredients:

2 eggs, whites and yolks separated

¼ cup butter, melted

2 tbsp. flour

3 tbsp. sugar

3 oz. chocolate, melted

½ tsp. vanilla extract

Directions:

1. Beat the yolks along with the sugar and vanilla extract.
2. Stir in butter, chocolate, and flour.
3. Preheat the air fryer to 330 degrees F.
4. Whisk the whites until a stiff peak forms.
5. Working in batches, gently combine the egg whites with the chocolate mixture.
6. Divide the batter between two greased ramekins. Bake for 14 minutes.

Blueberry Muffins

(Prep + Cook Time: 30 minutes / Servings: 10)

Nutritional info per serving:

Calories 178, Carbohydrates 26 g, Fat 7.6 g, Protein 2.9 g

Ingredients:

1 ½ cup flour
½ tsp. salt
½ cup sugar
¼ cup vegetable oil
2 tsp. vanilla extract

1 cup blueberries
1 egg
2 tsp. baking powder
Yogurt, as needed

Directions:

1. Preheat the air fryer to 350 degrees F.
2. Combine all the flour, salt and baking powder in a bowl.
3. In a bowl, place the oil, vanilla extract, and egg. Fill the rest of the bowl with yogurt.
4. Whisk the mixture until fully incorporated. Combine the wet and dry ingredients.
5. Gently fold in the blueberries. Divide the mixture between 10 muffin cups. You may need to cook in batches. Cook for about 10 minutes.

Cheat Apple Pie

(Prep + Cook Time: 30 minutes / Servings: 9)

Nutritional info per serving:

Calories 296, Carbohydrates 42.5 g, Fat 13.8 g, Protein 2.4 g

Ingredients:

4 apples, diced
2 oz. butter, melted
2 oz. sugar
1 oz. brown sugar

2 tsp. cinnamon
1 egg, beaten
3 large puff pastry sheets
¼ tsp. salt

Directions:

1. Whisk the white sugar, brown sugar, cinnamon, salt, and butter, together.
2. Place the apples in a baking dish and coat them with the mixture.
3. Place the baking dish into the air fryer at 350 degrees, and cook for 10 minutes.
4. Meanwhile, roll out the pastry on a floured flat surface, and cut each sheet into 6 equal pieces.
5. Divide the apple filling between the pieces.
6. Brush the edges of the pastry squares with the egg. Fold them and seal the edges with a fork.
7. Place on a lined baking sheet and cook in the air fryer at 350 degrees for 8 minutes.
8. Flip them over, increase the temperature to 390 degrees, and cook for 2 more minutes.

Conclusion

Still have your apron on? What are you waiting for? Throw it away along with your woks and pans, and try some of these amazingly delicious recipes the cleaner and much healthier way.

Now that you have convinced yourself that the air fryer is so much more than oil-free frying, the next step is to prepare these recipes, modify them to your liking, and create your own unique air fried delicacies.

DEAR READER

Thank you so much for purchasing this book. I've put a lot of hard work into making this a great resource for both experienced and beginner cooks and I hope you get an immense amount of value out of the book.

I know that not everyone likes to write book reviews but would you mind taking a minute to write a review on Amazon? Even a short review works and it would mean a lot to me and it will help me to improve and to provide a better quality product.

If someone you care about is struggling with anxiety or workaholism, please send him or her a copy of this book.

Finally, if you'd like to get free bonus materials from this book and receive updates on my future books, you can sign up for my newsletter at:

http://sixweeksweightloss.com/

Life awaits. Go #AirFry!

Made in the USA
Columbia, SC
10 September 2018